Conspiracy Theories

A Stunning Look at the World's Conspiracy Theories: Area 51, 9/11, The JFK Assassination, UFOs and Aliens, Corrupt Governments, And More

Cover image courtesy of Beckie – Flickr - https://www.flickr.com/photos/50066720@N03/5051540562/

Table of Contents

Do you want more books?

How would you like books arriving in your inbox each week?

Don't worry they are FREE!

We publish books on all sorts of non-fiction niches and send them out to our subscribers each week to spread the love.

All you have to do is sign up and you're good to go!

Just go to the link at the end of this book, sign up, sit back and wait for your book downloads to arrive!

We couldn't have made it any easier! Enjoy!

Introduction

I want to thank you and congratulate you for purchasing the book, "*Conspiracy Theories: A Stunning Look at the World's Conspiracy Theories: Area 51, 9/11, The JFK Assassination, UFOs and Aliens, Corrupt Government, And More*".

A Conspiracy Theory is a proposition based on clues that aim to narrow down the tunnel of investigation. It can also serve as an explanation to an unexplained event or a happening that is deemed dangerous for people, or an act that is illegal in nature. Often times, the one at fault (according to theorists) are a group of people, or perhaps, an organization.

While it is true that this book aims to entertain you into learning about some of the world's most compelling stories, it also desires to serve as an enlightening tool. With each turn of the page, your mind will be at work, constructing your own opinions, and weighing down the theories - what's reasonable? What's impossible? What's the truest of them all?

Most of the conspiracies mentioned in this book are already established: enduring theories that up to this point demand proof. Whether these theories are realistic or ridiculous, it's all up to you.

Before you begin your journey, please be reminded that each theory explained in this book is a mixture of fact and fiction. To avoid confusion, it will be clearly stated in the book whether a piece of information is reality, and whether it is an opinion.

Thanks again for purchasing this book, I hope you enjoy it!

Chapter 1:

Area 51

Conspiracy theories will not be complete without the mention of Area 51, but what exactly happened that a lot of mystery enthusiasts poured significant effort into to know more about the place?

What is Area 51?

Area 51 is also known as Dreamland, The Ranch and Groom Lake. It is said that this particular area in Nevada is just used to test weapons and aircraft, but if that is the case, why are all mystery (and UFO) enthusiasts so eager to find out the 'truth'?

Let's break the mystery one by one:

1. The establishment of this area is never known, and for decades people have no information that such an area existed. The secrecy even goes so far as deleting any satellite imagery caught. If they cannot be deleted, measures will be taken so that the public won't see them.

2. Although the US government kept saying that the

establishment of Area 51 was never a secret, every research made in the area is kept extremely confidential, and don't forget that they are hiding it.

3. The Roswell Incident. The mystery involving Area 51 will never be complete without pointing out what happened in Roswell, New Mexico in 1947. In the said incident, an aircraft allegedly crashed on a ranch in Roswell. Considering the supposed 'purpose' of the area, that is, to test aircraft and weapons, there should be nothing wrong with that, so what spiked the interest of many?

It was when Mac Brazel, upon the discovery of some of the aircraft's parts, mentioned that he could not 'fathom' the wreckages that had fallen. The military base afterwards released some conflicting information about the debris.

4. And the last of the mystery is this: it was only during the 1990s when the U.S. Government released an official statement. The debris found was from a balloon named Project Mogul, a top secret project that aims to dispatch microphones at a certain altitude where it can detect sound waves. Remember that the Roswell incident happened in 1947-- and the Project Mogul only lasted until 1949, why did they wait that long to disclose the information?

The theories...

1. The debris found was not from Project Mogul-- it was from an alien spacecraft and the secrecy was because the US Air Force is examining said wreckage. To make things more interesting, enthusiasts even believed that the alien life form (or forms) survived the crash, and the remains were kept hidden, again, for examination.

2. Some stories about the infamous 'Men in Black' were reported. Those stories say that anyone who was trying to uncover the top secrets of the government will be visited by the Men in Black, and they will be intimidated out of further investigation.

3. More intriguing theories suggest that the government is 'meeting' with the extraterrestrial life forms to create joint undertakings.

4. People assigned in Area 51 are finding ways by which they can manipulate the weather. If not that, there is also the theory that they are developing a technology that will enable people to tele-port or perform time travel.

Nailing the theories' coffin...

Over 6 decades of mystery and then it's over. To begin with, Area 51 is a military base, and it is not uncommon for military bases to be secretive as they often handle national security.

What truly nails the theories' coffin is the documentary by CNN entitled *Area 51 acknowledged, mapped in newly released documents*, and a very catchy tag line that says: *Area 51 is real, but sorry, no aliens.*

In the article, it mentioned that CIA finally released documents acknowledging the presence of Area 51, but not for the purpose most enthusiasts are after. It only revealed what other writers have already reported: Area 51 is truly a testing ground for weapons and aircrafts.

While this information may not satisfy the UFO believers, however temporarily that may be, experts say that this revelation is just the beginning. Perhaps we can expect more details to be disclosed about the famous testing ground?

Chapter 2:

9/11 Attacks

Perhaps one of the most tragic happenings in the history, the 9/11 attack has left a gruesome number of deaths, leaving a lot of families devastated.

Shortly after the incident, a lot of conspiracy theories surfaced, some of them are realistic, while others not so much.

In this section, we will compile the most convincing conspiracy theories about the 9/11 bombing.

1. It has something to do with trades

One of the most compelling conspiracies about the 9/11 attack is this: traders already know what will happen even before the attack commenced.

Upon investigation, it was revealed that a huge number of put options were placed on the stocks of United Airlines and American Airlines. These 2 airlines are the same airlines that were hijacked during the attack.

When a trader places a put option on a particular stock, it means that they will have the right to sell it just before the stock's value falls, thus, benefiting from it.

While it may be that they do not know about the actual bombing, it is still quite strange how the desire to sell stocks of airlines that would be involved in bombing, suddenly increased right before the incident.

2. There were bombs inside the towers

This one is a very plausible theory. Some survivors said that while they were attempting to escape the building, they heard explosions from inside the building. This suggests that before the attack, some bombs were already placed in several areas of the tower.

Furthermore, scientists proved that even though an airplane crashed into a building, its fuel should not be able to melt the steel frames of the towers.

3. How can you explain the Pentagon Attack?

If you look closely, the Pentagon attack can be deemed as the strangest of all the events that happened on the September 11 bombing. Reportedly, the Pentagon building was also attacked by suicidal terrorists on the American Airlines plane.

The funny (and weird) thing is this: the size of the hole created by the plane does not match with the plane itself. Flight 77 (the plane that crashed on the building) is 125 feet wide, the impact hole in Pentagon is only 60 feet in diameter.

What's more disturbing is this, unlike the crash that happened in the twin towers where people come and go (resulting in a lot of casualties), the side of the Pentagon that was allegedly attacked was vacant due to renovations.

Can it be that there really was no crash? Can it be that it was a staged missile that destroyed the vacant part of the building?

4. The theory about Flight 93

One of the heroic stories that surfaced after the attack is the story about Flight 93.

According to reports, the passengers fought as hard as they could so that the plane would not be able to crash into any occupied building, thus sparing a lot of innocent lives.

Instead of crashing on a specified populated building, Flight 93 crashed in Shanksville, Pennsylvania.

The weird thing about this story is the location of the wreckages. It was discovered that a huge chunk of the debris was found so far away from the major crash location, experts say that this may happen if a missile was aimed and shot at the plane at some point.

So, was Flight 93 purposely shot down? Some theorists are affirmative. They believed that the passengers learned of the plot so they couldn't be allowed to survive. Others claim that they survived the crash, but were murdered elsewhere.

5. Hijackers are there somewhere

After the 9/11 bombing, names of the hijackers have been identified, and upon inspection, they were found to be alive. There is nothing suspicious about it, seeing that the names of the hijackers are very common Arabic names (they said it was as common as John Smith in the US).

But what was really disturbing is the fact that passports of the hijackers survived.

How ironic can it be that the plane crash that destroyed the twin towers was able to spare the fragile paper documents?

6. Were the phone calls faked?

One phone call in particular brought a lot of suspicion--the male caller talked to his mom and introduced himself using both his first and last name. Who would do that?

The caller said that they were being hijacked, and when asked who these men were, the son just repeated what he already told his mom - that is "You believe me right?"

But one thing experts are certain of is this: those phone calls were fake.

The fact is this, at the height of 32000 feet, which is the typical height for a commercial plane, it is impossible to get any cellphone reception to send a text, much less, a phone call.

It was even studied, and truth be told, the success rate is less than 1 percent.

So how were they able to copy the voice of the callers? Experts say that there is a device that can record your voice for just a few seconds, and in no time, it can morph somebody else's voice into yours.

Up to now, none of these theories are proven (except for the phone calls), and due to these, the idea that the 9/11 attack is a huge cover up, is still well believed by theorists.

Chapter 3 :

The JFK Assassination

On November 22, 1963, beloved president John F. Kennedy was shot to death while parading in an open limousine in Texas. Speculations about his untimely passing surfaced and even when the government declared Lee Harvey Oswald to be the killer, theorists still refused to give in.

In this section we will take a look at the compelling theories about his assassination.

1. Death of witnesses

What made the assassination seem like it was not just an ordinary murder is the speculation about witnesses being intimidated or ignored. It was reported that a number of witnesses said they smelled gunpowder, but they were ignored by the Warren Commission (commission created to investigate the JFK assassination).

Some documents were also withheld, and even the films of the photographs taken by witnesses were confiscated.

Worse, it was brought to national attention that 103 people, who were supposed to be witnesses, died conveniently. Let's take into consideration Rose Cheramie.

Cheramie was picked up on November 20 by a lieutenant because she had sustained minor injuries from a car accident. During the drive, she mentioned that she would go to Texas. When the lieutenant asked what she will be doing there, she answered that she will pick up some money, pick up her baby, and kill Kennedy.

Alarmingly, the doctor who cured her (of her minor injuries) said that Cheramie also mentioned the knowledge of the JKF killing before the incident. When he reported it, the officer he talked to just said he was not interested. On September 1965, Cheramie was found dead on a highway, allegedly hit by a car.

An important note though, Cheramie was known to be a heroin user, and at one point in her hospital stay, she also mentioned to the same doctor that she works for Jack Ruby-- the person who killed the named killer Oswald.

2. Work of the Mafia

Before the incident, President JFK deported a mobster leader named Carlos Marcello after his brother was charged of creating crimes as a US attorney. When Marcelo found his way back to the US, he made threats toward JFK.

Some reports even say that he 'confessed' to the crime while he was in prison.

Many theorists believed this story to be true seeing that Jack Ruby was also connected with the mobster.

3. Connection with the government

A portion of the population also believed that the government was involved, particularly, the vice president during Kennedy's regime-- Lyndon Johnson. They theorized that Johnson had enough motivation: he wanted to become the president, and he allegedly hated Kennedy and was afraid that he would be dropped from the ticket for the next election.

Some even say that he was helped by wealthy people who felt that they would benefit from his presidency, and at some point even George H.W. Bush was theorized to have assisted him to do the crime.

Perhaps what solidified this theory is the fact that the Warren Commission (which ignored and intimidated witnesses, according to stories), was created by Johnson himself.

3. It's the CIA

When a murder happens, there is always the chance that the Central Intelligence Agency will be pointed out as the culprit. The JFK assassination is no exemption.

It was a well-known fact that The Bay of Pigs Invasion was unsuccessful and people believed that after such failure, a gap between the CIA and the president was formed, and this gap forced the agency to retaliate by assassinating him.

What made this theory believable is when it was revealed that the CIA *really did* plan some assassinations on certain people. A successful plot was that against the Vietnamese President Ngo Dinh Diem, and an unsuccessful plot was against the Cuban Fidel Castro.

4. It was Fidel Castro himself

The fact that the CIA plotted his death, makes it quite reasonable to think that Castro would want to retaliate. Even Lyndon Johnson believed it to be true. However, Castro's reasoning is also plausible.

At that time, any attack from Cuba would have been too obvious (seeing that the two country's relationship is so low), and also too dangerous. Remember how capable the US would be should they want retaliation.

Due to this, others claimed that the assassination was the doing of Castro's enemy-- in the hope that the US would pin him down.

5. Those who were around the president did it

As outrageous as it sounds, some people speculated those people who were around the president during the time of the assassination, to be the one who did the crime.

First on the list is Kennedy's wife herself, Jackie. Since Jackie was holding a bouquet of flowers, people said that she was capable of holding a gun and shooting it without anyone noticing. She was even rumored to be an undercover killer.

Second is the driver who was theorized to have been assisted by the man in the passenger seat.

And last but not the least, was Kennedy's bodyguard. This accusation started when an expert suggested that the firing was just accidental, and it was even published in a book entitled Mortal Error. However, it was proven wrong and the accused bodyguard even successfully charged the authors of the book.

The fact is, these theories are compelling, but the nature is very shakable. Remember that there were crowds during the assassination and they would have witnessed anyone of them (people near the president) pull out a gun and shoot Kennedy in the head.

6. Signal from the Umbrella Man

During the assassination, footage showed that a man was opening and closing his umbrella when the president's limo was passing by. The fact that he was carrying an umbrella is already suspicious seeing that it was not raining. Theorists suggest that it may have been a signal for the gunman.

7. The Babushka Lady

Footage showed that aside from the Umbrella Man, a Babushka lady holding a camera to her face never left the scene even when the crowds looked for cover during the shooting.

The Babushka lady was later asked by the FBI to step forward. A woman named Beverly Oliver showed and said that certain people asked for the film of her camera, which she had given, but they had not returned it.

Babushka is the Russian word for grandmother. Her outfit during the assassination consisted of a headscarf and a coat, things that a Russian grandmother would wear. She was also wearing sunglasses-- this made her face less-visible that some people even speculated that she was in fact a man in disguise.

Chapter 4:

Conspiracy Theories about Aliens and UFOs

Aside from the popular Area 51 and the Roswell incident theories, there are many conspiracy theories regarding aliens and UFOs. In this section we will discuss the world's most compelling, and therefore most believed theories about extraterrestrial beings.

1. The Majestic 12

The Majestic 12 or MJ 12 is a group of people in authority (scientists, politicians, and military personnel), that are said to examine extraterrestrial crafts. The MJ 12 also started on 1947 (same date of the Roswell incident), and was believed to be formed by the then president Harry Truman.

Revelation of the Majestic 12 began when certain documents were circulated by the UFOlogists. These documents were actually received in the form of film, that when developed, contained pictures of printed documents.

The documents contained some briefing for a so-called Operation Majestic 12. They explained how the Roswell incident was covered up, and how the space craft would be examined to obtain some extraterrestrial technology that they could utilize in the future. It also mentioned that they should consider being involved with alien life forms.

However, this theory was blown up when the government reiterated that the documents were just fabricated, and were in no way connected to them.

2. The Project Blue Book

Project Blue Book is very transparent. The government announced its two-pronged purpose: first was to identify if Aliens were capable of threatening the national security, and second is to further analyze existing UFO data.

Theorists believed that Project Blue Book was simply a cover up to redirect the people's attention from the Majestic 12. They said that although the project lasted for years, the efforts for the studies were very minimal.

In the end, these two pieces of information were disclosed by the Project Blue Book:

1. There were no Alien or UFO activities that will prove to threaten the security of the nation.

2. They have received over 12 thousand UFO reports, but upon further investigation, they concluded that most of them were cases of misidentification.

3. Ancient Astronauts

Perhaps one of the all time, and very plausible theories is about the ancient astronauts. According to this theory, aliens have already visited the earth and made contact to primitive people long before we had the simplest of technologies.

Some of the theorists believe that the extraterrestrial beings were the one who helped people built the world's strangest structures like the Pyramids and Stonehenge.

What's even more intriguing is the theory that those alien beings were the deities of the ancient times. They said that due to the very advanced technology of the extraterrestrial life forms, the primitive minds of our ancestors mistook them as entities associated with divinity.

4. The New World Order

The New World Order or the NWO is one of the most well-believed theories about Aliens and UFOs. According to this theory, aliens have always been with us - not just for a couple of years, but for thousands of years.

Theorists believe that the aliens are capable of shape-shifting into a very realistic human form. And with that ability, they are able to live among us freely, and without detection because the government are allegedly protecting them.

The main purpose of this cover up? Well, of course to take over our precious earth!

Chapter 5:

10 of the World's Most Compelling Conspiracies

From extraterrestrial beings, let us now focus on some of the world's infamous conspiracies that many people find compelling and believable. From cover ups to government corruptions, these theories will feed your mind and will make you ponder on the events with more enthusiasm.

Some of these theories have even endured decades, and clarity seems to be far from being obtained.

1. The Corruption in Turkey

Only recently, there was a massive Anti-Corruption Campaign held in Turkey and more than 50 people were arrested. There was said to be an overflow of evidence and most of those who were arrested seem to have a close knit relationship to the then Prime Minister Recep Tayyip Erdogan.

Some theorists suggest that there was really no corruption taking place (or if there was, it was not as big as what it seemed to be back then), and it was only the United States trying to weaken the Turkish government because they were simply becoming too independent and too strong.

Apparently, under Erdogan's regime, Turkey's economy thrived.

2. AIDS is a premeditated crime

Some theorists believed that the fatal AIDS that slowly kills its victim is a premeditated crime made by the US government, particularly the CIA, to wipe out gay men. Speculators do not believe that the virus originated in Africa-- they think that it was formed in one of the military laboratories in the US.

The process goes like this: CIA agents injected men from Africa with the virus using the Hepatitis vaccine that was in the testing stage before.

Same goes for other diseases-- some people think that they were deliberately manufactured so that vaccines can be created and people will be scared enough to buy them.

But is there actually a possibility that this conspiracy theory is true? Many believe that yes, it's highly probable. Let us first examine the *pronounced* origin of AIDS as *openly* explained by various health organizations.

According to the explanation, AIDS probably originated from a monkey, particularly, a chimpanzee. As some Africans prepared this infected chimpanzee, they might have received a splash of blood, and that blood entered their open wound, ultimately causing the infection.

However, a lot of articles have already disputed this "explanation". In fact, according to *Origin Of Aids*, that notion is impossible. Let us hear more about this:

Almost 15 years ago, *The Royal Society of London* held a conference: the aim was to debate, brainstorm, and tackle the real origin of AIDS and HIV. Renowned scientists from around the world collaborated and came up with the possibility that HIV was derived from a contaminated vaccine, which was given to numerous African villagers.

They concentrated their theory on OPV, or Oral Polio Vaccine; this is because OPV was partially created from the live, growing polio virus possibly contained in the monkeys' kidneys. Apparently, these cells were already proven to be contaminated with at least two cancer cells, hence it was definitely feasible for it to contain other viruses, like HIV-1, the deadliest, and most widespread various to ever befall upon mankind.

However, after serious debates, arguments, and

discussions, the scientists and researchers concluded that albeit the idea was possible, it couldn't have happened because they couldn't prove that those who manufactured OPV used monkey cells to produce the said vaccine.

Due to this, they had no choice, but to move on to a more conceivable scenario. Dr. Gerald Myers, from Los Alamos Laboratory in New Mexico, and who is also the US Government's Chief Sequence Analyst, reported to his colleagues the idea that zoonosis or the cross-contamination from animals to humans, couldn't have happened.

He reasoned that when AIDS begun in the mid-70s, lab results showed that there were at least 10 AIDS subtypes in Africa alone. How could there be ten types if HIV just came from a splash of blood from some chimpanzee? Dr. Myers said it must be iatrogenic, a disease which resulted from medical examination or treatment.

"It's not far-fetched," Myers concluded, "that 10 or so subtypes came from just a single animal, or perhaps a bunch of them caged together." But he said that "the vaccine hypothesis gives way to a more punctuated origin of AIDS".

So, as of now, we have two ideas: first, monkeys were not

used in the manufacture of OPVs, and second, AIDS could have been an iatrogenic disease. Hence, the only possible avenue to explain the origin of HIV/AIDS is if *other* (not OPV) contaminated vaccines were injected into the African villagers. The clues here are straightforward: the vaccine should have incorporated some chimpanzee cells, and it should have been provided near the time AIDS began, which is around mid-1970s.

The closest answer: Hepatitis B vaccine.

In his award-winning book, *Emerging Viruses: AIDS and EBOLA -- Nature, Accident, or Intentional?* Dr. Leonard Horowitz, a private investigator with a Harvard degree, showed some relevant proofs that the National Institute of Health used chimpanzees, which are contaminated with various viruses, in the production of hundreds of Hepatitis B vaccine which were distributed to the population of Central Africa ALONG with homosexual men from New York City.

Isn't it disturbing? To learn that educated and powerful people could manipulate someone else's health? That they could bring death upon hundreds and thousands of people with just a syringe and a promise that the vaccine will help them become immune to some sort of illness?

It's not yet proven, but we surely couldn't discount the possibility.

3. Paul McCartney actually died

To add music to our lists, let's discuss the infamous 'Paul is Dead' theory. The story suggested that McCartney of the very famous 'The Beatles' actually died in a vehicular accident that occurred in 1967. After that, some students in one Campus University gave emphasis to the clues, which of course, sparked the interest of a lot of people.

One good clue was about the Abbey Road album cover where the members of the band seem to be crossing the pedestrian lane. Theorists suggest that this cover seems like a funeral procession-- Lennon was dressed in white (the clergy man), Starr wearing black (the mourner),

Harrison in faded jeans (the digger), and lastly McCartney the only one wearing no shoes (the dead person to be buried).

More than these there were also accounts on hidden messages if you will back mask the tapes of their album.

Speculators suggest that The Beatles took someone who looked like him to pose as an impostor - if this is true, then the impostor is very much alive up to this date. Do you want to know more about the "evidence" that point to the fact that Paul McCartney died? They are listed down below:

1) In the cover of their album *Sgt Pepper's Lonely Hearts Band*, you can see a vibrant yellow wreath at the bottom right. The wreath was shaped like a bass guitar, which, many suggest was the Beatle's way to commemorate Paul, who by that time, had already been replaced by an impostor.

But the thing is, The Beatles fans said it wasn't for Paul, but for their friend and former member, Stu Sutcliffe, who died in 1962. Stu Sutcliffe was the original bass player, so when all the Beatles' members were given a chance to choose some famous personalities to appear on the cover, John chose Stu.

2) In the outro of their album, *Strawberry Fields Forever*, John Lennon could be heard saying something along the lines of "I buried, Paul." It was caught at the hard-left of the recording, so it's logical to assume that the cymbal microphone picked it up, perhaps because Lennon was near Starr when he said those words.

Again, fans who were steadfast in their belief at the band, defended the singer. They argued that at that time, the group was already aware of the death and impostor rumor, so it was highly likely that Lennon intentionally said those words to troll the theorists.

Later on, though, Paul himself (or his impostor?), said that Lennon didn't say "I buried Paul," rather, he said "cranberry sauce". Others suggested that he could have just said: "I'm very bored." Whatever the case was, that particular recording was still able to fuel the minds of many mystery enthusiasts.

3) Then, there was the infamous Billy Shears. In the *Sgt. Pepper's Band*, you can hear them introducing someone called "Billy Shears", and since then, people have assumed that this Billy replaced Paul McCartney.

The thing is, it didn't actually look that way, because when this Billy was introduced, it was Gringo Starr who sang the next line-- not Paul. The band indicated that during that time, they were under a lot of pressure. They came up with 7 best-selling albums and they didn't know if they could create another one, so to release some tension, they decided to get creative by "taking on" another personality. Billy Shears was, apparently, the product of that creativity.

4) Lastly, in the back masking of some songs *I'm So Tired* and *A Day in the Life*, you can hear statements like "Paul is dead. I miss him, I miss him," and "Will Paul be there as Superman?"

As intriguing as this back masking is, experts deny the claim. They say that *any* person could and would hear whatever they would like to hear if they just concentrate enough.

Paul, as the world all knows it, is still very much alive today. Or is it just the impostor?

4. Electronic Banking

Believe it or not, but some people believe that the use of

ATM cards (both debit and credit) is just a plot to completely remove money bills. The idea is once people are already very dependent on paperless buying, the 'higher ups' (whoever they are) will make a massive glitch that will cripple the electronic banking system, wiping out all the money that people have.

The end result of this theorized process? None other than to bring slavery back into practice.

5. The Mystery of the Bermuda Triangle

Since Bermuda has been taking away people, it cannot be helped if it will be included in the world's most believed conspiracy theories.

It is true that a lot of vessels went missing upon reported travel to the Devil's triangle, and it was also stipulated that compass glitch happens (theorists say that if you are in Bemuda, your compass will point you to the real Northern direction instead of pointing you to the magnetic North, which is the normal happening).

However, experts say that the amount of missing ships and planes in Bermuda is just the same, if not fewer, than other places. It's just that Bermuda is highly travelled.

6. Death of Princess Diana

Who can forget the tragic accident that took the life of the beloved Princes Diana? Ever since she was married to Prince Charles, people have come to appreciate her kind heart.

Unfortunately, her marriage with the prince did not last a lifetime and on 1996, they separated. 2 years after the divorce, the princess was in a vehicular accident that caused her death.

Theorists believe that it was really the Royal Family's doing-- they think that the Royal Family did not want the princess to marry her then boyfriend Dodi Alfayed, who is a Muslim. It was also speculated that she might know some deep dark secret about the royal family that made them force her death.

Another theory is this: paparazzi were following their car at a very high speed and it caused the collision.

7. The Tuskegee Syphilis Study

This is perhaps one of the saddest and most tragic cover ups in the history of not just politics, but of health care. In the study performed by the Public Health Service assigned in Tuskegee, 600 men were employed, almost half of them were already infected with syphilis. The problem? Half of the participants did not receive any treatment even though that was what they were told they would be getting.

Syphilis, once contracted, and not healed, can cause severe and chronic damages to the person's internal organs that may eventually lead to death. The good news is, a simple penicillin, which was already available in 1947, can cure it.

The bad news? The health care personnel didn't provide them with the cure, even though the study was conducted from 1932 to 1972. They could have easily injected the people with penicillin from 1947 onwards, but they chose not to. Apparently, they wanted to learn if syphilis would be better off without medication, and in their desire to learn, they used trickery and heartlessness.

They also wished to research about the effects of the disease, and they couldn't do that if those people would be healed. So yes, the PHS let 128 people die; 28 died from syphilis itself, while the other 100 died from related diseases. What's more, 40 wives and 19 children contracted the STD as well.

Broken down, there are 5 mean reasons why the Tuskegee experiment was unethical and illegal:

1. There was no informed consent. Informed consent is the procedure of asking for permission AFTER the patient or participant has been informed of everything there is to know about the experiment or method. The information should be provided to him in such a way that he understands every aspect from start to finish, including the advantages, the risk, and the side effects.

   In the Tuskegee experiment, the people were misinformed; to put it bluntly, they were lied to. First, they didn't know that they would be undergoing a research program—they thought that they were being given the cure. Second, they were not educated about the spinal tap procedure, which, even in the advanced medical world, is still regarded to as a dangerous method.

   In other words, this lack of education gave the participants no choice. They thought they would be getting all the good, and none of the bad, so why would there be a need to reject the offer? Had the professionals only talked to them honestly, many of them would have declined.

2. PHS "forced" the participants' hand by saying that to have the cure, they needed to sign an agreement which allows the health department to conduct an autopsy test on their body. To add insult to the injury, they said that if they signed the agreement, then their funeral costs would be covered.

   The lure of cure and death insurance was very appealing for the participants, who, in the first place were illiterate and impoverished black men. It was as if the people from PHS held the men at gunpoint.

3. Cure was denied even though it was readily available. This, in itself, was illegal and unethical—an outright declaration that PHS wasn't pro-life.

4. The health department used misleading advertisement. The slogans said: *Last Chance for Free Special Treatment*. Again, there was no treatment, but they made the slogan in such a way that people wouldn't be able to resist the offer.

5. It was a reflection of discrimination. Back then,

> PHS believed that the study would be able to help humankind, but they failed to include the welfare of the participants and their families—as if they were not part of the "humankind". Was it because they were black?

In the end, this cover up was blown and the US government paid the survivors of the family a sum of $10 million dollars, and a lifetime of *real* health care.

Chapter 6 :

Fake Moon Landing

Almost 4 decades and some still speculate that the moon landing by Armstrong is nothing but a hoax. According to speculators, the US government before, was so hell bent on beating the Russians in the arena of space exploration that when their attempts failed, they resorted to shooting the moon landing.

Theorists suggest that it has been directed by Stanley Kubrick, and that it was very much possible because in 1968, a film with an almost similar setting was featured in his movie A Space Odyssey. Two theories surround this “filming” suspicion-- first, the US Government had approached Kubrick after his 1968 film because they saw how realistic his work was, and the second was that he was “groomed” to perform the specific task of faking the exploration and that the film was just a “practice” for him.

Enthusiasts looking for subtle signs were quick to identify clues from Kubrick’s film, *The Shining*. In one of the scenes, the child was wearing an Apollo 11 t-shirt, which for the enthusiasts, was an indication that Kubrick played a part in the said mission.

The second clue was the line seen at Jack Nicholson's typewriter paper -- the statement says: "All work and no play makes Jack a dull person." For many non-believers, the "All" actually stands for A11 or Apollo 11.

And to add more fuel to the fire, the waving flag sparked into a wild fire because there should be no wind in the vacuum outer space. How come that flag is waving? But to NASA's defence they said that it was the force of burying the flag that caused it to move-- not the wind.

Theorists even believe that the three astronauts who died during the equipment testing for the first mission were actually executed because they were about to report the truth. If you need more proof, then they are outlined here for you:

1) There was no crater on the surface after the space module landed. Enthusiasts believe that the spacecraft should at least have left some kind of "blast crater". In all the photos released by NASA, the surface under the module looked undisturbed, as if the craft was simply placed there without trouble. However, they (NASA) insisted that there was no gravity on the moon, and because of that, the impact wasn't that hard compared to when something would land on earth.

2) The shadows. Everyone is aware that on the moon, there is only one strong light source, and that is the sun. Because of this, it was logical to assume that all the shadows would run parallel to each other-- however, that wasn't the case.

In some photos featured by the administration, it showed shadows spread at different directions, indicating that there were numerous light sources. This, according to many, was proof that the moon landing happened on a film set where stage lights could be placed.

As much as a believer would want NASA to indicate that they had brought their own light source, they didn't. In fact, when presented with this theory, they tried to blame the uneven terrain of the moon. But as expected, the words were barely out of their mouths when people started throwing their defence to the trash-- for really, how could uneven terrains cause shadows to fall at different directions?

3) Astronauts should have died. According to many people who officially and unofficially studied space exploration, the astronauts should have been cooked while traveling to the moon. Apparently, before reaching their destination, they would have to pass through the Van Allen Radiation Belt-- a radiation-packed streak held

in place by the earth's gravity.

NASA had argued time and time again that although the astronauts indeed traversed the belt, they didn't stay there for a long time. The craft traveled at a speed which made it possible for the spaceman to receive only a little radiation. On top of that, they said that the interior and exterior of the module was coated with layers upon layers of aluminum.

4) The hanging object. In a close-up image of one of the astronauts of the Apollo 12 Mission, critics became astute in pointing out the object which was reflected on the spaceman's helmet. The object appeared to be hanging, but no one could make out what it was. Others were quick to assume that it was one of the lighting sources, but to this day, no one knows for certain, for even NASA's side on it was unheard of.

5) Perhaps one of the most compelling (and convincing) arguments over the genuineness of the moon landing was the apparent lack of stars. If you'll look at the photos taken by NASA, not one image featured a shining star -- the space around the earth and the moon was completely dark.

https://en.wikipedia.org/wiki/Apollo_11#/media/File:Apollo_11_lunar_module.jpg

https://en.wikipedia.org/wiki/Apollo_11#/media/File:Apollo_11_Earth.jpg

This theory was not something that NASA handled well; in a lot of people's opinion, they only offered an "excuse". When asked why the space was without even a piece of star, they said that it was only the quality of the images that prevented them from showing. To put it simply, speculators scoffed at them-- there were many good quality photos released and yet it still showed no part of the many constellations. Besides, even photos taken here on earth can capture stars, so how come they couldn't?

Believers of the fake moon landing suggest that NASA left them out intentionally because they couldn't figure out how to map the stars in the setting. Remember, stars are in a certain position, hence, if people could ascertain that their position were wrong, the cover would be blown.

6) The rock formation with the letter "C". Believe it or not, but one of the featured rocks from the moon came out with a perfect "C". The way it was "written" was so perfect that it couldn't have resulted accidentally. NASA had given conflicting remarks about it: first they said that it was probably a mistake of the photo developer, or he purposely included it as a joke, then later, they mentioned that it could have just been a strand of hair which was unintentionally included while the photo was developing.

7) Edited background. Things got even more intriguing when two photos were released and NASA said that they were taken miles apart-- one photo featured the space module, while the other had none. The problem? When one image was plotted above the other, it clearly showed that the backdrop was the same. From the curves to the cast shadows-- it was identical. Theorists contended that it was because the administration merely edited the

photos, and in their desire to release many photos to show the world, they made a mistake.

NASA of course defended their side by saying that the moon was just smaller, so it was easy to see everything in a closer perspective.

With all these clues, it's impossible not to have some doubts. Still, let's take into consideration one thing - the astronauts who landed on the moon brought home hundreds of rock samples that were verified. Or were they not?

Chapter 7:

We are Headed by Reptiles

If it is not aliens leading us, then they could be reptiles. Like the New World Order theory, the Reptilian Leaders theory suggests that shape shifting reptiles are among us, and they are known to be very influential, like the Queen Elizabeth herself.

The proponent of this theory, a BBC former reporter named David Icke, even published several books about it. In his books, it was mentioned that these reptile leaders are the people, ugh, reptiles behind powerful organizations such as Illuminati and Freemasons.

Due to his efforts though, David Icke earned the title “Paranoid of the Decade” in the 1990s, but was he really paranoid, or there was truth in his theory?

Who is David Icke?

David Icke, born in Leicester, England, had a simple life. His childhood was filled with football games, so it wasn’t surprising that he made a career out of sports during his early adulthood. Unfortunately, he developed arthritis in the knees, which got worse when it spread all over his body.

Right then and there, he knew football was already out of his options, so he shifted his attention to sports broadcasting. Before long, people could see him delivering athletic news in BBC radio and television.

In the 80s, he started exploring other possible options to cure his worsening arthritis, so he researched about alternative medicine. Around this time, too, politics -- especially the Green Party -- picked David's attention. Hence, after getting fired from BBC due to tax issues, he concentrated on being the influential leader of the Greens.

Things began getting interesting for David then.

He claimed that during those trying times, he was awakened: David realized that a "presence" was around him, and that this "presence" was trying to convey some kind of message. Perhaps in his need to understand these messages, he walked the path of spirituality, which eventually showed him some "conspiracy" theories that he hadn't heard before. After a spiritual trip to Peru, he quit politics for an undisclosed reason.

Loosened Screws

In 1991, David Icke did the unthinkable: he appeared on national television and told every one that he was being sent messages about an impending doom -- that natural disasters would strike the world and it would lead to devastation.

People were not receptive of his idea, but they did laugh at him and his family. He mentioned that during those days, a simple task of walking down the streets resulted in snickers from bystanders and passers-by: it was obvious that all of them thought that David had a screw loose. That ridicule, however, provided David with a sense of freedom. In one of his interviews, he confided that after he and his family received the worst of the mockery, he began to care less and less, until he reached the point where what other people thought about him didn't matter any more.

Hence, for the decade to come he spared no effort: he traveled and researched and he gave long talks to people about who really rules the world.

Reptilian Hybrids that Rule the World

To be fair, David's idea was not one of a kind; in fact, it

has been mentioned generations ago. Many mystery enthusiasts already embraced the notion that aliens were already among us, and that they had been watching all along. They wanted to infiltrate the government so that they could be powerful -- powerful enough so they could turn us, humans, into their slaves.

David's theory was just a little more advanced.

According to him, the rulers of the world are divided into some sort of class, giving the people some illusion that they are divided by race, country, religion, preferences, and careers, but the truth is, all these leaders are members of one team-- specifically one blood line.

To prove his point, David asked: what are the odds that all 44 US presidents have French or European Royal blood in them? From Bush to Clinton to the current leader Barrack Obama-- they all shared one lineage. Could it be that public voting isn't about the public at all? There was a battle, sure, but the winner wouldn't be the one who garnered the most votes, but the one who had the highest percentage of royal gene.

Worse, David added that the carefully intact bloodline can also be found on other powerful people, even in those who are not in the field of politics. Examples of these powerful people are bankers, pharmaceutical company owners, food industry tycoons, and even actors and actresses!

For instance, some of the most renowned Hollywood actors and actresses like Tom Hanks, Marilyn Monroe, Brad Pitt, and Madonna all have royal descent. Coincidence? David thinks not.

He indicates that our world today is ruled by two things-- money and power. Money comes from banks and businesses, while power descends from fame and leadership -- this is why they don't just focus on government and politics, because they knew that it would take more than that to conquer humankind. When asked how this "secret ruling" was possible, David said that it was because these reptilian leaders had the power to manipulate people, even DNA.

When did this happen? Probably a long time ago-- David claimed that at one point, the reptilians had entered our world and they began "interbreeding" with humans-- perhaps not physically, but certainly through manipulation. This was why, according to David, people have "fundamental reptilian genetics" within their brain.

In the long run, this interbreeding process produced hybrids which could understand more than ordinary people could. They had more advantage, and because of that, they were more useful. These hybrids scattered all over the world, knowing in their minds that they are far more superior than the rest of us.

They became the Royal family, the leaders of the dynasties, and the powerful businessmen. David feels that this was why the royalties often want to “keep it to themselves”-- so that the genes wouldn’t be diminished.

Behind Closed Doors

In his talks, David also revealed about the annual close door meetings of global leaders; he said that instead of talking about economy, terrorism, and climate, the rulers perform rituals which most people of today would identify as satanism. “They follow a religion that dates back at the beginning of the civilization,” David added.

Chanting, sexual activities and blood sacrifices are just some of the rituals performed behind closed doors-- and any one who develops an intricate plan to uncover these activities would be silenced. Take for example, John F. Kennedy. Apparently, in one of his famous speeches, President Kennedy attempted to reveal the goings in the secret society. A portion of the exact quotes were as follows:

"The very word "secrecy" is repugnant in a free and open society; and we are, as people, inherently and historically opposed to secret societies, secret oaths, and secret proceedings. For we are opposed around the world by monolithic and ruthless conspiracy that relies on covert means for expanding its means of influence..."

David also revealed that the Catholic Church had played a large role in this expanding influence; to make it more convincing, he pointed out Pope Benedict XVI's resignation. David claimed that it was probably because the pope was blackmailed after he released some information about the Catholic Church's homosexual activities and child abuse involvement right within Vatican. Was there proof to this claim? Apparently, there was.

Neil Brick, a victim of this abuse, even founded SMART Organization in 1995-- SMART stands for *Stop Mind Control and Ritual Abuse Today*. Neil asserted that each year, thousands of children are thrust into the heart of Vatican to have their minds manipulated so that they would perform sexual activities and they would be more receptive in the idea of torture.

Worse, these secret meetings happen in different places around the globe like the bizarre gathering that happened at the Bohemian Grove in California where in about 2000 members of the "elite" united for the "Summer Festival"-- but in truth, they were performing inexplicable acts. The said event was infiltrated by Alex Jones, and you can watch it on YouTube.

What do you think? Grasping David's theory is not something someone would prioritize, but you must admit that he showed some solid arguments.

Chapter 8:

The Effect of Subliminal Messages

According to some experts, marketers have a way to our subconscious minds that make us more submissive into buying their products or using their services. According to the theory, subliminal messages in the advertisements do not enter our conscious mind, but it stirs something in our subconscious that makes it receptive to the idea of what is being advertised.

The idea is to advertise something else (something that people will like) in a very non-noticeable fashion. People then will buy the product, but not because they like it, but because they saw something in it that they liked to have. The most popular theme in the use of subliminal messages is 'sex'. Why? Because sex appeals well to people.

What exactly is a subliminal message?

The concept of subliminal messages is actually simple: if you *don't* notice that an item is being advertised, then you will be more interested to have that item. Experts explained that subliminal clues do not get recognized by our conscious mind, however, it can be perceived by the more powerful sub-conscious. The most effective techniques to insert these messages are through audio or visual ways.

For example, in a movie, you may not see a product being shown openly-- but it was there. The advertisers or promoters insert appealing words, phrases or images in between the movie frames so fast that you wouldn't even be able to read or notice them. But make no mistake: the sub-conscious part of the mind was able to catch it.

The perceived pioneer of this subliminal advertising, James Vicary, claimed that he was able to persuade people to buy popcorn and Coke after he inserted some subliminal clues in a movie. Apparently, in the said movie, James added phrases like "Drink Coca-Cola" and "Hungry? Eat Popcorn!"-- After the movie, the sales of the two products skyrocketed.

When people heard of this "effect", some sort of mass hysteria developed. As expected, people did not like being told what to do, hence, the thought of being manipulated without them knowing about it was abominable. They believed that these subliminal clues, whatever they were, could be used to attain political power, thus, the conspiracy theories about it were born.

The only problem? James Vicary lied to every one-- he didn't really perform the experiment -- he just told a scientific fraud. So, does that mean that there was no such thing as mental conditioning through subliminal clues?

It doesn't.

Subliminal Messages Are Real

Despite the fact that James Vicary's experiment was a hoax, a 1999 study performed in Harvard concluded that subliminal messages may just be true. In their research, they asked a group of people to enter a room and play computer games.

Unknown to them, the games were incorporated with a group of words-- one set was with positive words like "accomplished," "astute," and "wise" and the other set had negative words like "dependent," "senile" and "diseased".

Those words were shown very quickly-- in just about a thousandth of a second -- so it was impossible for the participants to have read them. Surprisingly, the gamers who were shown the positive words left the room faster than those who were shown the negative words.

Why are people scared of subliminal messages?

In reality, people are not really scared of the messages--they are, in truth, scared about the possibility that they could be manipulated into doing, feeling and buying things. This is because the subtleness of the messages makes them flexible: they could be inserted even in the most innocent of songs, movies, and photos. Take for example, Disney movies and animation films.

As we all know Disney films cater to children AND family-- they provide colorful stories with moral lessons, they are child-friendly, and for the adults, they are entertaining. It's easy to assume that people from all over the world would welcome a film so long as Disney created it. However, what if in doing so, you are exposing your children (and yourself) to subtle messages that could affect their and your perception?

For instance, in one of the scenes in *The Lion King*, when Simba, the main character, collapsed at the top of the hill, dust flew to the sky and discretely formed the word "Sex". Then, in one of the episodes of *Aladdin*, Aladdin was heard saying "Come on good kitty... take off and go..."-- nothing was wrong with this statement, however when some critics analyzed the episode, they found out that in the muffled background, Aladdin was really saying: "Good teenagers, take off your clothes".

Needless to say, a lot of parents were outraged. Another example that we cannot forget was found in "The Rescuers," wherein, in one of the scenes, there was a poster of a naked woman. The poster was slightly blurred, but was distinguishable; it was also shown very quickly, but critics were still able to catch it.

That movie was first released in 1977, and because of the outrage of the people, Disney recalled at least 4 million copies. When the film was remade in 1992, the company insisted that they had removed the poster. The question is-- why was the poster included in the first place when they knew that the film should be child and family friendly?

On top of these sexually related subliminal clues, Disney was also accused of providing discriminatory messages. One of the most famous examples is the scene in *The Little Mermaid* wherein the Jamaican-speaking crab, Sebastian, sang the song *Under the Sea*. The lyrics go like this:

"Up on the shore, they work all day

Out in the sun they slave away

While we devotin'

Full time floatin'

Under the sea..."

Parents suggested that Disney was trying to pollute their children's minds with the idea that living a non-working life while others are slaving off is the definition of the good life.

Aside from *The Little Mermaid, Dumbo* was also traced with some kind of discriminatory messages. In one of the scenes, black men and animals were working at the circus while singing the song which said: "We work all day, we work all night, we never learned to read and write, we work all night, we work all day, and can't wait to spend our pay away."

Worse, if you look closely at the workers, they had no facial features-- as if to say that they were not important enough to have distinguishing characteristics.

Now the answer to the question, why are people scared of the subliminal messages, is obvious. Just imagine millions of children being thrust into the idea of sex and discrimination without them knowing it-- without their parents knowing it. That's just plain scary.

Why are subliminal messages inserted?

It's a difficult query to answer, but most believers think that subliminal messages are used to control the world. In Disney's case for example, they are accused of "preparing" the youths for the New World Order.

Worse, various people pointed out that Walt Disney was a part of the infamous Illuminati-- you can "prove" this by just looking at the logo of the company itself: you'll notice that "Walt Disney" had three, 6-like figures shown in an almost straight line. In most culture, 6-6-6 is the symbol of the devil. Additionally, their most famous character, Mickey Mouse, is often portrayed wearing a witch's hat with glitter around him, as if he was casting a spell.

And Disney is just one company who uses subliminal messages. There are others, perhaps, thousands.

Chapter 9:

The Holocaust Didn't Happen

https://en.wikipedia.org/wiki/The_Holocaust#/media/File:Selection_Birkenau_ramp.jpg

https://en.wikipedia.org/wiki/The_Holocaust#/media/File:Nazi_Holocaust_by_bullets_-_Jewish_mass_grave_near_Zolochiv,_west_Ukraine.jpg

Despite the fact that it made worldwide noise, tension, and outrage, the Holocaust didn't really happen. Well, at least that's the opinion of people who claimed that the Holocaust is nothing but a hoax. This theory is called "The Holocaust Denial"

What is the Holocaust Denial?

Holocaust Denial is the claim that there was no Holocaust-- that most of the Jews who died in WWII, died not because of gas chamber, torture, or forced labor, but because of poor nutrition and other diseases. The rest of the Jews who were able to stay alive where in fact relocated -- not killed.

Of course, this idea isn't that famous in the United States: only 2% of the population disbelieved the happenings in the Auschwitz camps. However, a whopping 28% of people in the Middle East believed the Holocaust Denial to be true. The denial was so widespread that many European countries ordered that denying the Holocaust was to be punished by law. Did you know that one British bishop found himself being excommunicated by the Pope because he stood by his belief as a Holocaust denier?

This idea wasn't something that just came out because someone wanted attention-- it came out because deniers had some grounds. In fact, even famous historians, like David Irving, denied the existence of the Holocaust even to the point of creating a 2-hour documentary about it.

One of his arguments was the gas chambers. As many of us know, these gas chambers were used to poison Jewish prisoners with the use of cyanide (or other poisonous gas). However, David claimed that the chambers were not for people, but for the clothes of the prisoners.

The deniers, also sometimes called revisionists, said that

it was possible that the Germans were really planning on "getting rid" of the Jews because for them, they were inferior people, but they indicated that the "Final Solution" was not massacre, but rather, a simple deportation.

Even Hutton Gibson, father of the famous Mel Gibson, said that the genocide didn't happen and that it was mostly fiction; he claimed that Jews just scattered all over the world. How come they welcomed this idea but not genocide? Revisionists said that it was because no signed document about the genocide was found, but there was a pending agreement which showed that the Germans were considering using Madagascar as a relocation place for many Jewish families.

Proof

But does the lack of documentation invalidate the countless proof which point that the Holocaust did happen? Certainly, it doesn't-- but revisionists have more to reveal. Below is some "proof" that the extermination in many concentration camps didn't occur:

1) In Eli Wiesel's book entitled "Night," he narrated the happenings in Auschwitz camp during WWII; surprisingly, not one thing about gas chambers was

mentioned. Sure, the book was just over one hundred pages, but something as drastic as gas poisoning should have been included if it was rampant in the concentration camps. What's more, at the end of the book, when Eli was given a choice to retreat with the Germans or stay under the wing of the Soviet Union, he chose to retreat with the Germans.

2) The Holocaust was said to have claimed millions of people's lives; if that was so, then there should be tons upon tons of dead bodies or skeletons. But no one found anything. There were dead bodies, true, but not 6 million. Believers argued that the Nazi's burned the bodies in the hope of covering their massacre up, but if that was the case, there should have been thick ashes. Again, there was none.

What's more, after the rescue of the Jews, the Auschwitz camps were only accessible to the Soviet Poland until the 1950s, so it was highly possible that the "evidence" had already been altered, or worse, planted.

3) At the height of Auschwitz massacre, there was US intelligence in the area. This was because the Auschwitz camps were where synthetic rubbers were produced. If gassing was happening in the camp, then why did the US intelligence not report it?

4) Many post WWII books by renowned wartime leaders didn't mention genocide. Some of these leaders were Churchill and Eisenhower. If the massacre by gassing was so pronounced, how come they failed to relate the story? Unless of course, gas poisoning didn't happen at all.

5) History says that the Holocaust claimed 6 million Jews-- but according to statistics, for that to happen, each female Jew on the planet must have given birth to at least 13 children! Although females are capable of giving birth to multiplc children, the population census performed by the Jewish community themselves didn't report that kind of fecundity.

6) Perhaps the best argument the believers have is this: the Germans themselves admitted to the genocide. However, revisionists clarified that those admissions were brought by torture: in the famous Nuremberg Trial, the German soldiers were held captive by their (mostly Jewish) interrogators.

7) Lastly, the biggest enemy of deniers is when believers ask: why would people need to lie about the Holocaust? A normal person wouldn't be able to comprehend why a person or a group of people would lie about the entire thing, but revisionists say they would if only they understand about the motivation. The motivations, according to some deniers, were financial compensation

and social advantages.

Up to this day, Jewish people are still receiving huge monetary payments due to the perceived suffering and deaths of family members. Since they are known to have suffered more than enough hardships, people from around the world would forever see them as victims, and because of that, they would be bound to receive favors in terms of treatment.

If the Holocaust is just a hoax, then how come many people have been fooled?

People do not like getting fooled. If you went by someone and told him that you lied to him, he might never see you in the same light again. Most of the time, a person has a "detector" when it comes to what's true and what's fabricated; so how was it possible to lie to almost the entire world without getting caught?

A Chinese proverb explains this using just one sentence: A lie told a million times will become the truth. Perhaps, the most powerful of the Jewish communities really plotted the Holocaust hoax so that the odds would be in their favor in the coming future.

It could also be that they hadn't thought about it until

they noticed that the Germans' greed could be used against themselves. And when the opportunity presented itself, the Jews seized it. Whatever the reason was behind the deliberate plotting, the revisionists knew that the gassing at the Auschwitz camps were unreal.

The Verdict

The verdict quite falls to the believers' side -- that is, the Holocaust **did** happen and that the Nazis killed approximately 6,000,000 Jews. You may be thinking, how did that happen when the items above clearly presented the Holocaust as a big lie? Simple: there is more proof in the believers' favor.

The first proof of course, was the corpses of 1,000,000 Jews found in various pits. Aside from the corpses, there were also documents that the people behind the mobile killing units prepared themselves. They had all the death tolls and the details, like how many were men, women, and children.

Now revisionists would say that those documents were forged, but that's highly unlikely. First and foremost the reference markings on the documents matched the typewriters used by the Germans.

Second, these thousands of papers were found in various archives all over Europe and lastly, all the right files were in the right sequence. If those documents were forged, the Jews did a very good job in a very short period of time.

But what's going to convince you that these documents were not forged was the fact that deniers were and are still looking for the proof that the Final Solution was ordered and signed. If the Jews were capable of intricately forging thousands of documents, why not create a proof for the Final Solution?

That should be easier-- just one document to be planted somewhere in one of the archives to be seen by all. But as it was, there was no such document, forged or genuine.

Second point: the confessions. Deniers insist that those who confessed were tortured-- and to be honest, they had a point. Germans knew that a confession from them would result in the death sentence, so they probably wouldn't have admitted their crimes unless they were under duress. And if a person was under duress, then his or statement was not valid.

However, revisionists failed to point out that most of the confessions were written AFTER the perpetrators were sentenced to death. They were going to die anyway, what's the point of confessing? Unless of course, they were telling the truth.

And of course, the most obvious proof that the Holocaust did happen was the disappearance of countless Jews. Now, many revisionists would say that this proof is dismissible -- those Jews who disappeared didn't die, they just migrated somewhere else, like in the Soviet Union and United States, where there were already a lot of Jews, so an addition of a couple of million more wouldn't make a noise.

In this light deniers actually reasoned that those who disappeared never reconnected with their pre-war families because they had a bad life (marriage).

It was a valid point, but don't you think it certainly wouldn't happen to millions of Jews? What's more, gassing buses were real. At least that's what valid evidence suggest. In a letter written by Dr. Herald Turner, chief of the German Administration of Serbia to Karl Wolff, chief of Heinrich Himmler personal staff, he mentioned about shooting any Jew that he could get his hands on, and then he saw a "delousing van" and found it effective, hence he expected that they would be able to "clear the camp" faster.

Some letters from other officers even suggested that they could “improve” the buses by decreasing its size-- that way, it would be easily manoeuvred on the roads and when it was packed full of people, there would be no “waste of space”.

From letters to physical evidence, it showed that there was gassing in the camps; there was torture and there certainly was a death wall. Believe it or not, but the Germans even tried to cover their tracks-- still though, due to the large volume of proof, it was an impossible task.

Even Anne Frank’s Diary was questioned, but a thorough investigation revealed that the entries were genuine.

As it was, the Holocaust was a historical tragedy that’s been widely accepted not just by Jews, but by the people who helped refugees and those who sympathized but couldn’t do anything. Although the evidence on the genuineness of the Holocaust is huge, it’s comforting to know that there are people who are brave enough to go against the flow-- who are willing to do their investigation because they wanted the truth.

Whether the tragic series of events happened or not, it's undeniable that the Holocaust is already a part of world history.

Chapter 10:

William Shakespeare Isn't Real

https://en.wikipedia.org/wiki/William_Shakespeare#/media/File:Shakespeare.jpg

Another part of history is William Shakespeare-- the man behind numerous plays like *Romeo and Juliet, Hamlet,* and the *Sonnets.* People knew him well -- his books were printed a million times and his kind of writing impressed both literature enthusiasts and laymen. You might not have heard of it, or perhaps you did, but there are some people who think that William Shakespeare **didn't** write the infamous plays.

How they came up with that, we'll find out.

Just recently, a movie entitled *Anonymous* was released in different theaters; it was directed by Roland Emmerich, the man behind suspense films like *Independence Day* and *The Day After Tomorrow.* The film, which didn't gain much popularity, was about the possibility that someone else had written Shakespeare's works. According to the film, the plays were written by the 17th Earl of Oxford, Edward De Vere, an aristocrat in the court of Queen Elizabeth I.

Now, make no mistake - it doesn't mean that Edward De Vere was the only contender; there are others who could have been the man behind Shakespeare's famous works. Various authors were taken into consideration, but only Edward De Vere, Francis Bacon, and Christopher Marlowe made the cut due largely to the "proof" which we will discuss later. As many enthusiasts reveal, there are at least 50 candidates.

Also, the film is not the sole basis of this Shakespeare denial; in fact, the confusion on William Shakespeare's authenticity has been going on for almost two centuries now. It was probably due to the lack of evidence that the man existed.

Did you know that aside from two portraits, there were only marriage records (to Anne Hathaway), few signatures, a 3-page will, and business transaction records to prove that William was a real human being? What's more, the business records were not even related to writing! There was no record of schooling, and there was not a single manuscript to be found.

Even famous people doubted Shakespeare's authorship; some of these authors are Mark Twain, Henry James, Charlie Chaplin, and Sigmund Freud. Mark Twain said that Shakespeare of Stratford "never wrote a play in his life," while Henry James was convinced that "the Divine William" was the biggest and most successful fraud in our patient world.

If Shakespeare was indeed a fraud, then perhaps, Sigmund Freud was spot on when he said that not knowing who the author of the great comedies, tragedies, and sonnets was is “such a shame.”

Proof

1) The first and perhaps most valid proof was the fact that there was no playwright named William Shakespeare. To tell you honestly, evidence suggested that the documents, which we have mentioned earlier, belonged to an actor named William Shaxper or Shaxpere who was born in Stratford-upon-Avon. If you happen upon an academic scholar and he mentioned William Shakespeare, then remember that they are talking about the actor-- not the playwright.

To add fuel to the already blazing fire, records prove that Shaksper’s parents, John and Mary, were illiterate. Even his wife, Anne Hathaway was illiterate. Even their children were illiterate. If this actor was indeed the man behind the theatricals, then he would be the only famous writer who gave no mind to the literacy of his children.

Shaksper also had no records of ever going to school, and to put it bluntly, it was as if he didn’t really write; while other writers like Voltaire had thousands upon thousands of letters and correspondence, William Shaxper had zero.

2) The second piece of proof was the known fact that

"Shakes-spear" was a popular nom-de-plume. Back then, people were keen on using this pen name because it represented Pallas-Athena, the Greek Goddess who always carried a spear. Works like *The London Prodigal*, *The Puritan*, *The Birth of Martin* and *The Comedy of George Greene* were credited to different Shakespeares.

What does it say then? It only means that back then, there were **many** Shakespeares. It was possible that another man wrote his plays.

3) Third, his immense vocabulary. Mind you, Shakespeare's Canon had more than 29,000 different words, making him the man who knew the most English words. Did you know that *Paradise Lost* written by John Milton only had 8,000 different words? And then the *Holy Bible*, which was translated by 48 of Great Britain's most knowledgeable Biblical Scholars, only had more than 12,000 different words?

How could a single man, who had no proof of formal education, have used 29,000 different English words with coherence, ease, and emotions?

4) Mark Twain's work, entitled "Is Shakespeare Dead?" tried to debunk the idea that there existed a man named William Shakespeare by explaining how no one lamented

over the death of the Bard of Stratford. Apparently, when the infamous Shaxper died, there was no noise in England, not even in Stratford! How was that possible, Mark Twain thought; does that mean that Shaxper was not a famous playwright? If he was, then there certainly would have been tributes, memoirs, and poems of appreciation to the man who created heart-wrenching and moving plays. Mark Twain based this on the fact that other celebrated writers like Francis Bacon and Walter Raleigh were appreciated at the time of their death.

The conclusion? Shakespeare didn't write the famous plays.

5) His strange will. As what was mentioned earlier, William Shakespeare left a 3-page will (some reports said it had 4 pages). There are several strange things on his will: first, it was his attorney who had handwritten it; you would think that as a writer, he would have done the writing himself, but no -- his attorney took care of it. Second, he never mentioned anything about writing: someone who was as passionate as the Bard of Stratford probably would have included something about his works, like who would take care of the manuscripts, and the unfinished works, but again, nothing was mentioned. Lastly, someone as knowledgeable as William Shakespeare could have owned hundreds of books. Knowing this, one would assume that he would take care of it by including them in his will, but he didn't.

Did he not include his books in the will because he had none? For many non-believers, it was likely. During the 18th century, an extensive search of every book case within 50 miles of Stratford was conducted in the hope that authorities would find the books belonging to the famous playwright; however not a single book was recovered.

6) Did you know that William Shakespeare was well-versed in various languages other than English? The playwright was well-known for his fluency in French, Italian, Spanish, German and Greek. How could William Shaxper, a man who was virtually surrounded by illiterate people, have possibly learned all these languages without education or even books?

After knowing this proof, we will now move on to the possible candidates. These people could be the real William Shakespeare.

Sir Francis Bacon

One of the candidates in terms of qualification is Sir Francis Bacon. As a man who studied in Cambridge, and as someone who traveled often, he certainly could have acquired the correct knowledge and skill to write the various plays. Aside from being a philosopher, Sir Francis

Bacon was surrounded by many literate people, especially since he was a member of the Privy Council and he held the title of Lord Chancellor.

The first person to ever raise Sir Francis Bacon's name as the possible Bard was Delia Bacon -- no relation. While most people only doubted Shakespeare's identity, Delia announced Francis Bacon as the alternative author. However, she argued that he didn't write all those plays alone: he must have written them in collaboration with other renowned authors like Sir Walter Releigh and Edmund Spencer.

When asked why they needed to hide their identities, Delia indicated that it was because they had "political" agendas. She claimed that inside the plays were codes that reprimand the government for their lack of action to the haunting issues of society.

Christopher Marlowe

Already a known playwright, Christopher Marlowe certainly had the qualities of a literary genius. The thing that made him a strong candidate was the fact that his works, when compared to William Shakespeare's works, held many similarities in patterns and style. The comparison was not just made by people, but also by computers.

Another point for Marlowe was his biography, which hinted that he was a spy for the Crown. This gave him a reason to hide his identity. However, people identified that Marlowe died in a ballroom brawl in the year 1593, and that William Shakespeare's works continued to appear until 1614.

If he was The Bard, how could he have possibly written after death? Fans of Christopher Marlowe turned the tables and used this "death" to their advantage: they said that Marlowe didn't really die-- that he just faked his death because people were plotting to kill him. After escaping, he went somewhere and continued to write the plays.

Marlowe's candidacy as the real Shakespeare was featured in a documentary released in 2002, bearing the title *Much Ado About Something*.

Edward De Vere

Edward De Vere was a late candidate, but for the past 9 decades his fans have raised convincing arguments to the point that they became known as the Oxfordians. These Oxfordians have then become the most challenging "enemies" of the Stradfordians, or those people who firmly believe that William Shakespeare wrote his own work.

The first person to ever raise the idea was J.T Looney (pronounced as Loney). After his book, *Shakespeare Identified*, was released in 1920, thousands of supporters have emerged, including prominent personalities like Sigmund Freud.

The Oxfordians argued that since most of Shakespeare's plays have some "legal" discussions in them, it is only but logical to choose Edward as he was a well-educated lawyer. Not only that, but he was also a traveler, and the places he had been are the exact places found in Shakespeare's works.

For instance, in the famous play *Hamlet* – the main character, Hamlet, who the Oxfordians believe was reflective of De Vere's character, described himself as "set naked" in the kingdom after he encountered some buccaneers. This scenario was similar to Edward De Vere's kidnapping; apparently, the Earl, while traveling the English Channel was kidnapped by pirates and was left naked in Denmark Shore. Let's not forget that Hamlet was "The Prince of Denmark".

Another interesting "proof" was the presence of the characters Rosencrantz and Guildernstern. In the play, these two were the Hamlet's childhood friends, summoned by King Claudius to determine the cause of the prince's madness, and if possible, help stop the insanity.

Guess what? De Vere's brother-in-law apparently sent him a letter, describing how he went into a banquet together with two courtiers named, you guessed it, Rosencrantz and Guildernstern. The Oxfordians argue that the very letter was a private correspondence.

Oxfordians also believe that Hamlet itself was a play about the Elizabethan Court, which De Vere was a part of. In fact, many characters resemble a real life person: Polonius, for example, represented William Cecil, Lord Burghley, the trusted advisor of Elizabeth I, who was reflective of Queen Gertrude's character.

Then, let's not forget that in the play, Hamlet was enamoured with Polonius's daughter, Ophelia. Guess what? In real life, Edward De Vere married Anne, the daughter of William Cecil.

Many Oxfordians believe that Hamlet was an autobiographical play created by the Earl of Oxford to expose the happenings in the Elizabethan Court. And because of this, the play itself was treasonous, hence, the need to hide his identity. They point out that if De Vere didn't use a pen name, then he wouldn't have survived the laws.

William Shakespeare

But of course, let's not forget the side of the Stratfordians who believe that Shakespeare wrote Shakespeare. They concede that William Shakespeare might not have written everything on his own; that perhaps he shared the load with other writers, but this "collaboration" doesn't change the fact that William Shakespeare was real.

They agree that there was a significant lack of proof on Shakespeare's schooling, but at the same time, they said that *anyone* who ever studied in Stratford also suffered that same lack of documentation. Just because there were no documents, doesn't mean that there was no schooling.

This kind of argument got most Stradfordians bashed; for some disbelievers, they were holding on to something unreal just so they could continue earning a living through Shakespeare's birth, life, and "works".

Fans of Shakespeare argue on one thing, that, although a little unsubstantial, bear some weight: the works of Shakespeare was so “voluminous” that it was impossible to credit it to someone else. For, really, who could stand in the corner and watch all his works get credited to another man when he had poured his being into them?

What do you think? What theory appeals to you the most?

Conclusion

Congratulations on your journey to some of the world's most controversial theories.

I hope this book served its purpose to entertain you, and get your mind running about the unexplainable, the doubtful, and the reasonable.

Remember that these theories are not laid out in front of you to confuse you, but rather to add well-speculated ideas on your imaginative vaults.

Some of the theories mentioned will have to be laid to rest because of the proof provided, but it does not mean that there can never be more about them, so always be on the look out for updates.

If you enjoyed this book, would you be kind enough to leave me a review on Amazon? If you just search for this title and my name on Amazon, you will find it. Thank you so much, it is very much appreciated!

Do you want more books?

How would you like books arriving in your inbox each week?

They're FREE!

We publish books on all sorts of non-fiction niches and send them to our subscribers each week to spread the love.

All you have to do is sign up and you're good to go!

Just go to the link below, sign up, sit back and wait for your book downloads to arrive.

We couldn't have made it any easier. Enjoy!

www.LibraryBugs.com

Links to Images

Paul McCartney - https://www.flickr.com/photos/slagheap/2657548010/

Moon Landing - https://en.wikipedia.org/wiki/Apollo_11#/media/File:Apollo_11_lunar_module.jpg

Moon Landing - https://en.wikipedia.org/wiki/Apollo_11#/media/File:Apollo_11_Earth.jpg

Holocaust - https://en.wikipedia.org/wiki/The_Holocaust#/media/File:Selection_Birkenau_ramp.jpg

Holocaust - https://en.wikipedia.org/wiki/The_Holocaust#/media/File:Nazi_Holocaust_by_bullets_-_Jewish_mass_grave_near_Zolochiv,_west_Ukraine.jpg

Shakespeare - https://en.wikipedia.org/wiki/William_Shakespeare#/media/File:Shakespeare.jpg

Printed in Poland
by Amazon Fulfillment
Poland Sp. z o.o., Wrocław